SPLIT   INFINITES

Split Infinites

Rosmarie Waldrop

Singing Horse Press 1998

Acknowledgments:

Sections of this manuscript (sometimes in earlier versions) have been printed in *Abacus, Apex of the M, Avec, The Baffler, Bombay Gin, Caliban, Chelsea, Conjunctions, Grand Street, Issue, lin/go, New American Writing, No Roses, Notus, Object Permanence, Parataxis, Prosodia, Purge, Shearsman, Terrible Work, The Germ, Torque,* and in the anthologies, *A Glass of Green Tea with Honig* (ed. S.Brown, T.Epstein, H.Gould, Providence: Alephoe Books), *The Poet's Calendar for the Millennium* (ed. Douglas Messerli, Los Angeles: Sun & Moon), and *Trouble: Naropa Summer Writing* (ed. J.Schwartz and L.Gudath, Boulder, CO: Naropa Institute).

"Pre & Con" #3 has been a Hard Press broadside for Bernadette Mayer; #1 and #6 have been used in artist's books by Ann Slacik and Graziella Borghesi.

"Morning's Intelligence" was a chapbook from Salt-Works Press.

The author would like to thank the Fund for Poetry and the DAAD Artists Program in Berlin for their support at various stages of the writing of this book.

ISBN 0-935162-17-8

Published by Singing Horse Press
        PO Box 40034
        Philadelphia PA   19106
        (215)844-7678

Publication of this book was made possible, in part, by a grant from the Commonwealth of Pennsylvania Council on the Arts.

CONTENTS

PRE & CON
or
POSITIONS & JUNCTIONS

for Craig Watson

1

The sun's light and
is compounded
and lovers and
emphatically

and cast long and shadows
of and a look
and on the
and face of a girl

waiting for and
the night and with imperfect
repose and secret
and craving

and bodies operate
and upon one and
another and blue
may differ
and in depth

2

Of bodies
of various
sizes of
vibrations

of blue excite
of never except
in his early
in childhood has he touched

of the space of
between of
to allow
of for impact

now of that color
has slowed
its pitch
or of skin

of but light
no deep foundation
nor of leans into
the blue

3

When vibrations
when impinge on when ends
of the nerve

pure when reason
the aqueous pores of
when capillamenta

but children are never
when mentioned
only the blue when

fills the when night
when incomprehension
enters itself

as when a fleet
when of ships in
when classical times

never leaves
never when sight of
when land

for Bernadette Mayer

4

The biggest
vibrations with
strongest red

plum
blossoms
yellow peach

with a confusion
with all with white with
with brain

the right
conjunction with
loss a whole world

great mansions
in with ruins along
with the bay held

up by
their reflection in
with water

5

And possibly color is
divided
into the octave

gradations of
into love into
impalpable

in spite of into careful
attention into
leaves blown

into autumn blown
into tension into
between

growing into and
into ungrowing
desire into and into

6

If a bird if
up into the air
if cold if

we must if adhere if
a road if renamed by
if each if traveling

more than one set
if of darkness no angel
no annunciation

deeper yet if
the singer's
voice if

borne if by grief
as if a bird
if on wings

7

Figures how oscillate how
in search of
another how part
of the body

trick or treat cried
the kids
how thin how
unabashed

how a flaw
between how
I know how her scar
having slept there

small scar
how on a body of
how water too
how make love how

the surface unstable
how once
how upon

8

Vibrations that beat
and dash at the eye
at adhere

eclipse at
moved at at
feverish

at no matter at
how much we
at no matter no

matter how
at love we never
enough

9

As for the
explanatory

as art as relation to
death as and as
must negotiate

as time as and place
as fear allotted as

as silence that
as follows as dilates

an as great variety of
as noises in as
different

as makes me
as shiver

10

Or morbid
sensations or
understood to
or mean
like or invisible

currents or of
or thought from or one
person to
or another in
conversation

or purpose beginning
to develop to or
give the picture or depth
or so you
grow older

or traveling the or hiatus
or life and
a trembling
or in wrists and
or breathes

11

A molecule with
with Etruscan colors a
porous potential
with the threat the

with there
a language with
did not pass with
but away

yet exacted with great
from with ownmost
motion must be with
continued

by our nerves with
with brain where a with
takes you
with throat

12

But to scream but
our lungs are
but made for

"Now but is Night"
no doubt wrong
but let's but suppose

that a but sour wine
can yet and a man's
been but a machine but can still

but the approaching
chill
but prevents

CORNERED STONES

THE VITAL KNOT

APPLIED TO THE DESTRUCTION of cerebral parts. Signified weakness. Pulled the strings of his own puppet. A whir of cicadas emerged into the dream. A dripping faucet. All his life he had wanted a bicycle. Odd or even bodies of women.

Parts that excite. Wilted under the burden of response. An earlier state of things. Small like the start of a conversation. A gift for misgivings. Barely had he heard the first chords when he stopped eating.

Luminous motions. Cerebral lobes. Will, see, hear, remember, feel, annihilate time. Devoted to chance embraces, the inertia inherent in organic life. More fingers than he needed at the pleasure level still does not mean he recognized. A just-so story. The effect of music on animals.

The system was nervous. A ghost of himself, beset by unconsidered notions of the self. It took all of Mahler's rare talent to write his bad music. And now and then stomp, keeping time.

A point between the parts of feeling and the parts of movement, between flesh and mirror. Without the least guile, with all the conservative nature of living substance. He was all rhythmic agitation. The risk of losing not only speed, but his struggle to deceive himself.

A point very much like the collar between the stem and root of vegetables. Impressions must come here to be perceived. The rain, to beat down. Sincerity, to be interrupted. Suddenly women. Hooded crows perched on telegraph poles called to mind examples from animal life.

PLEASURE PRINCIPLE

OF COURSE IT'S NOT EASY to believe in your own dream. The working of instinct near water. Not orchards. Not apples or pears. Not nowadays. I don't know how psychoanalysis has no hesitation on how dark the night can get. The world, which is unfinished, occupying more and more of the sky.

Emotion as unpleasurable tension, the high passage of the moon. The laundry. Sensitivity won't do it. Therefore and quite often we lie down in stubbled fields. The voice of the cicada. Tells nothing.

Any day lies thick in the garden I propose to enter. Then fills with secret rivers that darkness feeds on. Lapsed sense of history. No massacre. The cicadas relentlessly.

It doesn't matter if your feet are small. When you're asleep. The fruit trees enormous. A motor idles in the foreground. If, with quicker travel, things did indeed turn out according to one's wildest. If a child could be born from something not a mother.

The circumstance that the wife occupies the inner room and rarely if ever comes out is called the pleasure principle. In certain societies. Suddenly made clear by the cicadas. The meaning of life, absolutely. Distinguished from the now moonless garden.

And hooded with fabric like mirrors not in use. And like appearance refusing itself. A pleasure that cannot be felt as such to transcend becoming strange.

An orchard in the foreground. With beginnings of unease immediately behind.

for Joan Retallack

LOCALIZATION

THAT THE PROPENSITY to steal has its own organ. Cerebral parts. Clean feet. Default: an apple tree all by itself. Explanation beside the joint, almost as far as the superciliary ridge. Fell into step. Fell into the hands. Hot weather firmly implanted in the pelvis.

Extending from the organ of cunning to unpleasant. Mere children of nature. Where unpleasant equals real life. Straw, rags, wood. Firmly focused on infinity without an inch to spare. Using the speech of other people, forgetting too much delight. The scissors must keep moving. Apples, apples, and apples.

Overcome by the unfortunate impulse, and at such a pitch. In love, in a black dress, not, indeed, in opposition, in the third person. Once the fear of flying catches in the spleen, a fierce need to sharpen scissors.

Propensity followed him into the cloister. In the name of science. To solve a powerful riddle by following the mistake into someone else's dream just as the wind comes up. Assault on the senses. Inflections, calm sumptuous syllables. Or barks, snorts, trumpets, roars, growls, rumbles. A condition called must.

She had looked in too many mirrors to experience experience as experience. A bite from the apple wrapped in snake. Nor can novelty, the condition of enjoyment, be denied her clandestine dimension. A mystery of pyramids and low-frequency calls. Surrounded on three sides.

The foot has its callus, but all creatures defend their nests. Innate adolescence. Risking everything, even intelligence. A riddle that distracts. Desperate to settle on a pronoun other than I. An unease with scissors until put in the pocket.

OUTERMOST

BEGINNING WITH: bodies move. "Carry themselves adversely." No image: mechanical concussions, railway disasters, the terrible war. Hard down to the payment. The living daylights.

Law of inertia. The puppet master straightens the most bewildering neuroses. To be swallowed red, but temporary. Wealth of motor symptoms approaching hysteria. The elephant's extremely sensitive trunk. The empty space inside the blind man now slated for demolition. Meticulous cross sections of muscle fibre.

If something is a body then it moves. Large populations. In front of trains. Separate paths to silence. Seeing, an involuted signal in the blind man's lungs. Or rather, vertical. Fright, fear, anxiety improperly used as synonyms for beginning, middle and end. And digest barely half of the rough forage devoured.

Does the proposition have to be expressed in the form "if-then?" If we know the puppet's imitation is next to naked. The train station, behind damage. Though an actual injury works as a rule against the birth of signs, the subtle blasphemy. Shoes, sticks, stones, consequences and graffiti. Gestation period up to 22 months.

Does it have to be expressed? In brief? In kilter? The light shut down tight. Useful knowledge: Sanskrit texts cast elephants almost exclusively in a military role. Mysterious adjectival energy. Swinging our arms while taking trains. We would hold on to blindness.

They will collide. Mating dance. Derailed trains. The terrible war. Later conceiving a child among run-down obstacles, wills, warnings. All that is left of inexplicably scattered is the child's sexual exploration. Pulling the string again and again. Just as the neck thickens into data.

But nobody would put it this way. Such harsh foreclosure. Such primary color. Such fatal complication of extremes. Kids on bicycles. Trains. But the outermost surface has ceased to have the structure of living matter, has become to some degree inorganic and resistant to the stampede of stimuli.

TO WIT A VERY SMALL GLAND

THOUGHT OF THE SOUL as joined to the whole body. Owing to the disposition of organs. Only afterwards he realized there was no map above the neck, no sin below the navel. Taboo equations. It was warm, the cortical layer without protection. Though if we displace the meaning of life inward in the persistent manner of a blind person, we are too. Without protection? At the bottom of thought.

Owing to the disposition of organs—the organs of the soul—if any one be removed the extreme heat of the sun floods the threshold. Insistent echo of eternity. Somewhere else. Instincts, representatives of bodily forces, he explained in passing. Even hours after waking up words from the dream invade our long childhood.

The dream enters the body as dream and hollows it for the soul. Only hours after waking up he realized and seemed suddenly older. Hesitant to penetrate the grassfire, decipher the mail, stress copyright. Lid effect. Still pressing forward with bruised knees, in the wake of eyes, like thinking without interruption in order to carry something back into sleep.

Only afterwards he realized that we can't conceive of half a soul. Any more than ignore nakedness. Bifurcation. Rain too enters the body. As rain. Unconscious point of impact. Pressing it home, which means warm claustrophobia.

32

No relation to extension, he explained in passing. Not smaller because some body moisture. Not inconsolable. Not naked. Not above. Owing to the disposition of organs, the body dreams with its tongue. With the persistence of a blind person. The eyes are thinking something else. Does this cause vertigo? Color separation.

Not the whole brain, he explained in passing, but its uppermost part. "This." Inasmuch as it is one, with enough anxiety to qualify as sexual. And the other parts all of them double. Warm without protection bound in flesh. Only afterwards he realized a person might still need to climb a mountain, if only in a promise, in excess.

for Pam Rehm

ACTION

"WHICH, IN THE BODY, is what passion is in the soul." So that naked. Deep water. Or the identical periphery of the dark. Rain enters the body. A baleful almost-music. Penetrating. Parts. The hinterland.

To hunt out the difference between body and soul in order to survive winter. And puberty. He played the piano. With a certain dampness. A long way from explaining the keys.

Congenital vertigo. Ferns, feathers, fingernails. All that we experience when we remove our clothes.

There is no shield against urges from within. The way thinking means hand in hand. We say all kinds of things to come more easily. Birthmark between thighs. The adolescent fear of green suspended.

Our tongues keep going. In circles. Impacted contact. "Wholly inanimate bodies must be attributed to our body." Cross my heart, my fingers, my path. Thoughts, easily with the river, and me pertaining to my skin.

I had misjudged the family members. Inflating pregnancy with bales of cotton, bundles of ribbons. The more endangered by folklore.

The naked part of morning disappeared. From one thought to every kind of hinterland. As much periphery and more children. Overly. Religious opposition carved into ivory and difference of age. Piano keys. Another man undressed according to techniques we've learned. Not a matter of emerging nationalist movements.

Parts became rare. Our bodies filled with tears. The fog was penetrating.

CORNERED STONES

SCRAPING AWAY mortar is easier than moving the stone. End of not started yet. White, furious, surplus, paper ribbons. Mercury rising.

Wish-phantasies vary according to latitude. The way humidity clings. A wild beast under the melody. To bulk the score. A couple screwing neither here nor there.

Ego throws anchor in megalomania. Against calligraphy. Symptoms of composition. Take a girl for a ride. Reckless gauze. Super-id.

Assembling old materials into new shipwrecks. A joke like green lacquer. It's not just that we can't solve the problem, but it slips through our fixations. Fear of flying in the ointment. Major fog.

But "this is true" does not necessarily mean "this is how it happens in China," in a heatwave, in cahoots. Up to our necks.

Getting off light. Now that women. Magnetic border. Waists not squeezed between whalebone and the obscure apogee of night. Riot of telescopes. Only temporary prevents seeing.

No one is ahead of his time, and he only slightly.

Ideograms on paper ribbons. The Id withdraws into the Pacific. The deeply, but nevertheless inhuman process of seduction. Beads of sweat. No cure for behavior. Wild parade with key.

We cannot escape the history of construction. From what other source derive old age? We make no claim, for the moment, to know the origin of air. Only slightly less anxious.

THE SPEECH CENTER

THE THIRD CONVOLUTION on the left had softened. The house burned down. Later, all perspectives were pale, gritty, gray. Certain fishes overtake laborious migrations. Back beyond childhood. A countryside so vast and every year more so.

Though he had lost his speech, the air was full of dust. Old saw. The same applied to birds of passage. A saturation of mothers. Ratio of retrieval by crook of contentment. An itch to hook back boundaries.

His tongue was free. He could move it anywhere. And stretch it out of his mouth. Myself as well. In conversation up to my elbows. But no talent for lack. Him plunging a knife into his own revolt.

No words down here. A sense of organs destroyed: the insula, the striate body, the frontal lobe. Looking for them in all the bars. Obliged to recapitulate between asides. Once again he would assume a spiritual state of patience. Which is then a pleasure. Even if the particles don't go at the center of the flag.

We must not only study the damage, but also punctuation to slow down reading. The phenomena of heredity. The facts of embryology. The rare albino. Instead of proceeding to behavior and domicile, keep an eye on impoverished. On holes in the sentence.

The lesion being progressive. Fare limit. Margin of not replaceable, of at the mercy of. Clash of. Blot out. An attitude, a gesture, a step, a stumble, a fall. Gnarled levels. Legs. Less.

DECOMPOSITION

THE MATHEMATICIAN admires a theorem. The factory whistle blasts off. He eats a filet of smoked eel. Paranoia decomposes just as almost without a pause. As though a natural phenomenon.

He sees no need for baths. Or, rather, paranoia resolves once more into their elements the products of rapidity and startling. The crowds push. The crows fly. The wind ows. It's marvelous, he says. Though to lose oils would be to rob his body.

Lost the green thumbtacks. Irritating, annoying, stimulating. A representation of caught in the rain. With the wonderful properties of numbers, the shadow of a pear.

The constant warmth of the decomposing process. So rolled up in a ball, in the sense of trouble for the undertaker. Shoes too tight, schematically.

Absurdity in dreams abbreviates abuse. But beauty never fails anyone. Steamed dumplings. Old age.

As though he were admiring regularities in a crystal. Therefore dissolution not occuring. A frameless square of mirror.

Regardless of the number of doors, the monotony of the solutions provided by psychoanalysis. Picture nailed to the wall. Number theory in private spasm. Once again, symbolism overrides grammar.

REVERSALS

DISSOLUTION BEING PARTIAL. To the most complex, least organized, most voluntary. Summer at eye level and changes character with different speeds. How little agreement there is on death. There being a war. The bellies of birds in flight. Looking is difficult.

Taking to pieces with fingers so long. Thoughts of female self-gratification. From natural causes. He rolled over in the dark. Many animals pass through. The construction mysterious. Evolutionary currents. We will have to eat less. The surface dimensions of dawn. A thought coming in great pain, in the flesh.

And never ceased to move. No term for indeterminate gender, for inversion of gravity. Animals backstage. With extreme art. With the acidity of dawn. Because looking intently is difficult. Soot gets into the cracks.

After a number of divisions the infusoria become weaker. True or false? He let out a cry. Dawn precedes the perception of dawn. Bone needles. Needless to say stones are harder. And it's possible to look intently without seeing anything. There being a war. In the presence of all the animals.

The brain as openwork knitting: just one little stitch dropped. Meeting his own reflection in the unstable dark he went both ways. And fainted in the wake of his own blood, you follow me?

Local dissolutions in cohesive logic. A ripple deep in the mirror. A sea-urchin egg, segmented. He sat up in bed. Looking can tire even when you don't see anything.

DIRECT STIMULATION

IT BEGAN WITH irritation. Inside him. A face that corresponded to his idea of long. Provoking a lost organ, an absolute yes. It was then exaggerated. By taking an archaic attitude. Or leaving it. His listening. And chewed eagerly.

Eye movement of a sort. Face created by rage for love. So his self was quite unknown. Did he have one? The tension that then arose, invariably. Flushed with readiness, sniffing his armpit, smashing into the subatomic race. His listening with understanding. With difficulty. With a crankshaft.

There being a group of weak muscles. The word was stimulation. Touch stone. The child dismembered the clockwork. More naked than latent. The instinct to return to the inanimate state. The vocative. Snow.

More deeply into the center. Without discovering his past life for sale. Dig. Spin. Strip. Collide. Begin. The green of pierce. Proportion of person to perturbation. So strong his eyes could not translate it.

Back, tail, stomach muscles. Scrambled script. The chemical structure of the young. Furiously and therefore. Useless tear (con)duct. How to be genetic. With information of our own. With coffee in cracked cups.

The nerve of the facial. As if to act it out would recreate the feeling. As if water consisted of hydrogen and harsh. Remorseless light on remote areas. Face red from the wind.

VIGILANCE

A PEN AGAINST the force-field of reflex. Rapid weather. Old wounds. The tasks of air. Apart from sex, a lucky charm in someone else's pocket. The hands of biologists. Around the waist, presence is attenuated and the past shows through.

Many aptitudes such as shooting never reach a high degree of perfection until the necessary movements are carried out unwittingly. Blind graft on kneejerk. Taste of nothing in the mouth. The concept of death slides down the barrel. The cement takes on consistency.

How to stretch voluntary muscles as far as the Mediterranean when the reflexes reach such marvelous complexity in damp climates. She wanted to mend his clothes. Eat steamed dumplings. Hear music in the middle of a clearing. Age in the female voice, moved by the richness of what exists. Ends of yarn. Pebbles. Bus tickets. Plenty of animal forms.

Reverse punctuation. Repressed instinct never ceases to strive for the perfect dividend. Muddy boots. The tone of flexor muscles pricks no ear. The vigilance with which the higher neural levels activate tattered maps. Where time runs back on itself with sufficient distance we advance into the buried incomprehensible. They wrote in knotted threads suspended from small sticks. Midden splendor warped with silence.

A ball of thread equals solution. Animal hair, leaves, pods. Woven sun. The compulsion to repeat stored in a closet. He concentrates on his socks. Thrust himself into her surprise. Inextricably. The needle moves through the labyrinth, the pen across voltage levels. Ways of knitting the world, surreptitious news in the air. And almost walking on it.

for Edwin Honig

SPLIT INFINITES

ASSOCIATION

NO SOONER does one appear than the next comes at a smart pace down the aisle, bent on a game of love, and sometimes crying. I'd prefer the single exclamation. To stand small, insubordinate, in the sea of fertility.

Are you sure, she asked, you're talking of ideas? Dark emptied of touch would be entire, null and void. Even on an island.

Explosives. It was war. There were no condoms. We swapped knives to peel off childhood like so many skins. Cause, far from being opposed to pregnancy, is in truth the most exquisite species of proximity in time.

Electricity through interruptions in the countryside. Practice of blindness. Clipped fingernails.

A nudge between thighs. The weight of a single egg. A single body multiplied into many instances of speculation. I ran up steps worn into a smooth path to motherhood. The motion as if natural.

If this streaking is disturbed we stumble, and consequence reveals its dimensions. Of which we are the sole survivors. Please clarify.

Techniques of avoiding Spain. Castles in. Of separating exis-
tence and essence. With tongue and teeth. A tight sweater
strips a single clockwise.

The toxic side of felt in the bones. And other couplings. The
pleasure of writing a poem. The slow behavior of stars. Does
not overwhelm the body.

for Claire Needell

51

A GREAT NUMBER OF ARBITRARY SIGNS

AND A DEEP discontent with variable wave lengths. The shining dandelions had already bloomed into puffballs. The air apparent, flickering with heat.

Light cannot turn corners. The steep program of the pleasure principle. The splash of the fountain. Fingers on arteries practicing scales and arpeggios.

While concepts lay unobservable in the brain, the leaves began to fall. During the blackouts, the city gave in to the dark like any countryside. A wide space of hearing, but free from entanglements with fertile soil. And like lovers knew the time that was given and the time we must take.

The way the fountain braids my listening after sparrows, swallows and soldiers have been broken into phonemes. And the waves pounding the achievements that are wedged between our lives. One cup poured into another makes different animal ancestors.

What is important? The body of water itself? The sublimation that makes civilization possible? Mother lit candles and kerosene lamps.

Soap not necessarily a source of happiness. Marrow of water. A fountain's sound is changed by the slightest gap in the air.

Love draws its orbit through the heavens, while the land beneath heaves with calamities. I lifted the blind and looked down on the color of war, now lost. I might not have known all the meanings of red sky at night.

The light has turned the corner. When sublimation comes to rest the jet of water falls back upon itself. As if the fountain itself were under water. A sleep incautious and entire.

SPLIT INFINITES

A SMALL SQUARE with tram lines in several directions, bounded on one side by a church. Attempts at recollection succeed soonest with corresponding sepia. I myself cannot discover any "oceanic" feeling within me. Adding up dark cobble stones against more unguessable events.

Lilies with heavy pollen powdering priestly fingers. Indiscriminate application of adjectives. The next day my throat was swollen. To the extent that sex is in the mind I threw snowballs.

The towers of the church rose into red shifts. The snowflakes drifted slowly in the opposite direction. God blesses those who are careful. Not to step too far into rejoicing.

We'd done it twice already. Mother moved slowly with a small hook. But the longing for the father is incontestable. You feel a splinter and you don't know where it came from.

Narrow rooms. When we say infinite we have no conception but our own inability. Therefore the name of God is used. The I has no sharp boundary inward.

A train of thought departs. Spokes of the mind wheeling backward. Exhausted, the light. Erased, the fine line of the horizon.

Snow drifted in under the door. The iron stove glowed red. Tense flesh of lilies thick to the touch. All receding, toys drawn on a string.

Roma quadrata. Inaccessible, he says. The embryo cannot be proved from adult lips blue with cold. Memory not regenerated in the marrow.

Rising from the grass, the trees, the park, many obscure modifications of the spiritual life. Tumbled garments, faded photographs. The bodily forms of light can't be looked at face on. The snow continues to fall.

MEMORY SCAN

NOT THE GREEN MOUNTAIN embedded in strong feeling I expect-
ed. More an exaggeration of fog than German poetry. The iris
expands to the vast range of beasts. The focus not tamed down
to meet a repertory of formal signs. Calculus meaning stone
and used for counting. Not applicable. Dark reek of bliss.
Ready for. The tasks of culture.

An inlet, a very small clear center lost amid cobwebs. Light
smooth as fruit. Ready to bite and sin, original. Pebbles wet,
weeping willows, poplars, plum trees. The fog vast sweat. The
sun too, mute. Because of the distance, a terrible thirst for
love. Six thousand years ago, pictographs of trees, sacks of
grain and heads of cattle. And the nature of the moon, its light
borrowed at interest.

Looking at a picture of the landscape is easier than looking at
the landscape. The past, upon scrutiny. Not just postwar
focus, but deep and fetid. Interval eclipsed. By fog misunder-
stood as bird and egg, shadow by shadow. Once father and
mother dissolve: dragonflies, mosquitos, missing ribs? The sign
for hand in the upper right corner perhaps indicates owner-
ship. Culture gives us these ideas. Depending on the number
of chambers in the heart, trepidations of the flesh.

To understand the full clearing as the young animal turns human. Coupling curiosity with upright for speed. Hands become intelligent, economics, incorporated into body temperature. Not necessarily for the best. Raw blood, urine, faeces transformed into resemblance, contiguity and cause. And the more sensitive but sparser rods. Condition of anxious suspense converted into the tongue as home. Still, strangeness makes us shiver and retreat inside the skin.

Balked in my simulation of childhood. As consciousness flakes off, the animal soul plunges into haze. Relation of didn't perceive to didn't happen. Coercion and trimmed fingernails. Does the right to despise those outside our culture makes up for the wrongs we suffer in it? Several strokes descending from heaven meant night, the principal language of Mesopotamia. Here, as in dreamlife, curiosity nestles into the fur. From humble beginnings as an accounting system. So rich a store of clay envelopes on arms raised toward gods most apt to fail us.

MEMORY TREE

AND SECONDLY, in German.

My first schoolday, September 1941, a cool day. Time did not pass, but was conducted to the brain. I was taught. The Nazi salute, the flute. How firmly entrenched, the ancient theories. Already using paper, pen and ink. Yes, I said, I'm here.

I was six or seven dwarfs, the snow was white, the prince at war. Hitler on the radio, followed by Léhar. Senses impinged on. Blackouts, sirens, mattress on the floor, furtive visitor or ghost.

And mother furious. Sirens. Hiss. The cat. My sister cried unseen. Her friend. Afraid to look. What did I know of labor (forced) or pregnant? The deep interiors of the body? I had learned to ride a bike.

The black cat. The white snow, the blue flower. A menace of a different color. Uniform movement with unsurpassed speed. Not fastidious. Not necessary for substance to be filled in deep inside.

Mother, I cried, extremely. And wolf. Exceeding the snow I was at home in, wool pulled over my eyes. O wolf. The boy who did not cry it also died. Twilight overtures.

Face fair. Black hair. Hands parsimoniously on knees. A Polish girl. In Germany? In the war? Moving along swiftly in the air between us, a continuous image. Enough of black cat panic, bells (hells, shells), of sirens, hiss of bombs.

*

A long life of learning the preceding chapter. That my soul in bluejeans, my mother in childbirth, my rabble of hopes in German, East of expectation, West of still waiting. In bed with an antidote.

Eating of the tree. Leaves falling before the fall. Through a hole in memory. The fruit puckers new problems, but doesn't quench. The orchard long-abandoned.

THE MIND

SAID MY FATHER. A door open, a gray carpet, a flat dampness. A cat. A field. The means of power and coercion without which no civilization. How to possess oneself. He thought he had explained. What does "I'm frightened" mean?

A black cat. A field. All the colors of memory, however crumbled. Power, discourse, and legs. Spread in a dance too normal to stop. At pains. Not naturally fond of work.

The sun still there, the moon already in the pines. All hands in the field. Women and prisoners. War internalized as everything. A father is a father, but the super-ego is monosyllabic. The nature of touch under wraps and, like the world, folded. Can it appear in another connection?

If you tell me you're in love I understand a different order of window. Nothing avails against passion's ungainly, but luminous. Trapped in a sleepwalk. The cat both by the woodpile and in the past.

Grammar aligned according to race. Too bitterly other and taught to respect. Surplus of privation. Polish. Yiddish. Prisoners in the field. Of wheat. The cat with its sleek black pelt. Tactile parts of body. In what context? In the field, harvesting.

Let us therefore use a little nubile and strong. Bewildered, carnivore. And that from childhood. Mother in a pose of annihilation. Sexual autonomy. Does it occur? Cf. *Philosophical Investigations.* To the ends of the earth.

A simple cat by an ordinary woodpile. The body with pain and difficulty. With wallpaper of chrysanthemums. And birds of paradise. With narrow windows and stiff-backed chairs. The mind, said my father. My father in the field. Of "honor."

Spasm out of a deep-shocked realm. One could also say: I simply say it. The mind, said my father. Opaque eyes. As if sick of seeing. As if decay were mining him under the skin. Reproachful, dissatisfied. Of course we find no answer.

Or only smoke. Who lit the fire?

DELTA WAVES

WAR CAME out of the radio before I had time. To scratch on a slate. Pictograms, phonograms, determinatives. The river's edge of marsh turned solid, the year, in on itself.

Cold oozed up through the soles. Shoes always too small, bending my toes. With so many absent, how to understand human nature. Delta waves: Disease, degeneration, death, defense.

Rhythm of sleep, of the first year of life. Brackish water thickened with soot and gum arabic. My legs itched in their woolen socks. Once again following an infantile prototype.

Obedience as a time of life. Not to lose essential speed in abstraction. In the long run, an animal god does not suffice. Removed from her setting, mother paced back and forth.

I too, for no reason, walked faster and faster. Everything was exactly as it seemed. Regions compressed by growth or distorted by injury. I was "thing" because "Rosmarie" required too much lipwork from a farmer's wife.

Wiping my feet became difficult. Speaking, even in cursive script, impossible. Swallowed up by deep woods. All falling still, all lapse.

I sat on one chair and then another. As if my thought processes had no practical motives. As if I were not wishing to be part of the family next door. What happens when the shoe is on another foot?

I thought lightning and thunder meant two clouds colliding. War, a surface to live on. A relationship fixed and never failing like cause and effect. Writing begins at the edge and rolls straight toward God (red ink).

Each slap revealed a face I had not suspected. The calendar changed from moon to sun. The frequency of rhythm more important than its amplitude. Or the squeak of my shoes as I walked to the blackboard.

On the other side of sleep the scarab came into existence. Hieroglyphs beautiful enough to be the writing of gods. With birds' heads pointing the direction to read them. A net of branches denser than the woods.

Sentences enclosing and opening out. Perspective changing endlessly around the interloper. In a fragmentary passage, I held a pigeon in my hand till the trembling stopped, but not the faint, rapid heartbeat. After such intimacy, how personify the holy ghost?

SNOW

SOMETIMES MELTS while the seven prismatic colors in succession produce the sensation of white.

Father told stories of poisoned apples, while mother's shadow fell ever so lightly. Then the Phoenician sailors traded the alphabet for solitaire, and brain rhythms grouped in broad frequency bands.

The dark edge of the woods receded into compulsion and custom. Still, muscles resist the encouragement of descent. No shelter from a brainstorm.

But a seeming mishap may avert nakedness. Natural space lost to mirrors on the wall. Depends as much on the play of light and shadow as on the marks of graver and chisel. Mother sat elsewhere in the body.

The chemistry of the brain must be continuously adjusted to flower prints from the calendar. Not like a ship in a bottle, but awkward trompe-l'oeil. With seven dwarfs or lean years. Their violation can be made good through washing with water. Or oiling the shotgun.

Words to be revered whether or not they can be understood. A compulsion as enigmatic as layers and layers of petticoats.

First remote foreshadow of a brainstorm as well as pubescent white lace apprehension. The impulse not abolished by portraits of ancestors. Or sleeping between impossible and unacceptable. The smoke is sometimes screened.

The language of the Etruscans has taken on the density of earth. Unsurveyed by geometers. Wherever two or three nerve cells are gathered together. Convulsive seizure of the day while lack of vowels drains out deep color. One after the other, mother refined the seven deadly sins. Wait until nothing is happening. Till the snow will not follow us south.

for Françoise de Laroque

"SHI," or: THE INVENTION OF WRITING

MOTHER WORE her shiny red boots with impatience. The power of commonsense disappeared through the black hole in the middle of the eye. Too many birds. The Emperor Huang-Che studied heavenly bodies. Eyes blue from watching the sky. Without compass, the tribes divided into totems and taboos.

I will now proceed with my explanation of how the margin is stripped to the last nakedness. How electrodes mean no more than the derivation of the word. How the Emperor Huang-Che studied bird and animal footprints. Members of the same totem are not allowed to enter into grammatical relations. At an angle into the blue depth of the eye. Mother thrust her chin forward so that the new violence would articulate space.

Forays in the blood where no oath could penetrate. The Emperor Huang-Che sadly waited for the tide to wash away his footsteps. The beauty of trees is useless, their representation tied to relations of production and power. If you count carefully, a comma. In the case of the mother-in-law, the rules of avoidance dangle modifiers. The Emperor Huang-Che discovered, after much study, that combining the characters for mouth and bird signifies sing; mouth and child, scream.

Grids of signs lock the planet. The Emperor Huang-Che wept through the night and, the story says, with much cause. The effect not so much related to sex as to pleasure. Not violent revolution, but native speakers. In a happy speculative mood, mother weighed mess against age, in against tension. The muscles in her neck stood out.

The scroll shows the Emperor Huang-Che wrestling with a block of ink. Because the Chinese characters have remained unchanged they have amassed a large number of meanings. *Shi:* power, world, oath, to leave, put, love, see, watch over, count on, walk, try, explain, know, be.

for Per Aage Brandt

THE SMOKE IS SOMETIMES LARGE AND COLORED

IT IS A NORTHERN COUNTRY. To which we apply close mathematical precipitation. Thought being a kind of locomotion, the subject is asked to describe exact change. A bed, a stool, a heavy-lidded from the night. Symbolic blood count propels a different satisfaction. But libido smokes outside while we talk. The work of writing. Not to embroider but out of the blue. With delight, the abbé Jaugeon locked letters in a grid.

Harsh, brief, poor. One word before other spatial ideas. Or the eye chart for boldness and freedom. Pushed sideways in time, desire quickens, even when directed toward a cut above. Yesterday was to the left. No wonder father's puny tobacco plants never got off the ground. Manuals by hand though an iron bed and copper plate would print large sheets.

Snow cargo. Intensive or. The process of scanning relaxes when the knife is found. Spinning and dizzy. After a trudge through our own vast emptiness. Every individual shows a mixture of biological sex with cycles per second. A union of activity and under water. Day follows day with the certainty initiated by the rotary press.

Rises from a complication of visual and tactile. To the attic. Used for drying the puny tobacco leaves on a string. The characteristic impression of interrupted. For example a knifepoint.

If you wish to understand you must follow the compact of clitoral excitation. Between elements of repressive, a staircase. How to write slowly like a man sowing a field. With mistakes. Absentminded in alphabetical order.

What happens in the brain after experience has done its utmost? Chair pulled to square eight of thought and personality? Even if we know about hope we must be present at birth. And puberty. Sit next to a new antenna for what never comes to be spoken. Later, tightly furled umbrellas. The hand for size and proportion. And an emphasis on speed love needs to come in writing.

in memoriam Poul Borum

COMPOSING STICK

THE WAY OF experience proper is the front door. Through the back, I carry my mother's body down into sleep. My mother lode. Ingrained vocabulary. I dreamed I was human, but not sure it was possible. I refer to the factor of actuality. There being ambivalence. Charlemagne signed with a cross, which he inserted into the loops of the signature prepared by one of his scribes.

Any form of thought a spasm of pleasure if we could get at it. Mother cleared my throat. My mother tongue. Where do you put your hands when constructing a hypothesis? Or inner stairwell? The brain must be able to communicate every item of information received in one part to all its other paroxysms. Sleep at a distance. Or following a fish. A sense of unease may afflict the traveler, but the scribe must retain a steady hand.

The tide of dreams washes up in the sink. Too many chairs, even at midday. Mother succumbed to the antique love seat. My mother of vinegar. And potatoes. If there is physical interference between these and the so-called silent areas, things are seen but not recognized. The tarot showed La Papesse, La Mort, La Tour Abolie. We may say that compulsion is beveled blindness. Initially, printing seemed more an extension of handwriting than characters moving toward a plot.

Often our discoveries come as lucky apples. Mother in a different constellation of confidential. My mother of pearl. On moonless nights surrounded by sobs. The mechanism for opening the eyes more finely tuned. Attention prowls among privacies. Furniture, pen, ink. A flicker of worry, dilapidated in its implications.

The exaggerated application of the principle of mere neighborhood. But many people can think better with eyes closed. The back of habit. Motherproof? House of cards. The projection of unconscious hostility greatly speeded up by the introduction of paper. After a pause, I practiced idleness. Down endless corridors, up winding staircases, the slow and laborious process of writing.

The elements of consciousness such as the glass reflects. Curtains, their capacity for surface. Feeling as big as the room, a child will dress up in her mother's clothes. My mother hood. Surely there are photographs to put in its place? An eyelid in the mind? When Gutenberg could not repay his debt, the banker Johann Fust confiscated all his material and hired it back to him. The hostility is cried down by an increase of tenderness, smoke blown into the room, or too sick for arrest.

for Gale Nelson

SEVEN SENSES

TOUCH

MORE COMPLEX THAN hands between thighs. But which is an adequate number of sons? And the different imagination of I'll have no descendants? As she comes, singing. Across the field, hope clings to her body. Birds. Quotation marks in the air. The knife, for a use intended beforehand. At a given distance, beginning with yes, the vocal cords vibrate, and the dying man knows how much time he has left.

The body, indeed, distinguishes. More than one set of darkness. But physical forces almost never create simple geometrical structures. Boundless hope, yes. The infinite comes wet, and a little death goes a long way. I turned, because. Even rough, fearless warriors swoon on this occasion.

Each sense has only one kind of object it discerns without fail. A fisherman in a garden? A woman on her back? No bird lives in my memory, I am sure. Wind in the branches or murmur of air conditioners. Difficult, the distinction between poetry and prose, sex and sucked to sweetness. As one yes, breathed, hugs another, the fury of lips and hips. Else, nothing. Thick drowning in the river.

The birds are clinging. Even though I stammer, the dog licks my hands. Breath. Beckons toward death. As against ships laden with perfume, shiploads of sheep. My sleep no shelter, my thoughts not pregnant, my most intense. But skin on skin, so salty slow, so heaped in summer.

for Emmanuel Hocquard

COLOR

DOES NOT INHABIT. Lies on top. The skin of the visible. A yellow tugboat, in wait. To catch the octave in the eye, the white of the mind. Opposite, the full weight of the sky. House steeped in blue Monday. Where certainty is continuous grey river clay underfoot. I walk and don't notice the strange leaps of the year.

Not dirty but deep. Yellow river sand. A sense of standing on brightness, saturation, hue. Evening, as if there were no other time of day. Color lifts off with the birds. But rooms need pictures to lean into. Still loves. A sphinx. Monks. Machines. Only dreams satisfy deep red.

Color in direct contact with the eye cannot be seen. Adjective under skin. House sealed in sensation. Whereas a transparent medium creates years under water. For impulse in all directions. The mind swims near the surface. Think. Of bluish orange. Clear milk. A grandmother painting her lips.

Once in a blue moon or note. The middle of the cornea introduces an erotic quality. Beyond marble tables, antimacassars, sphere of faded needs under the bell jar. If I had looked. Travels along the border of norm and experience. So that the meaning changes back and forth. No rainbow. Deep river witness. Closed lids against.

Drained by the long effort to see. Gray river clay. Pigment talks in your sleep, and a hush falls. Hardly an answer. In English? A yellow tug at the nipple. At comes between. If there were nothing, far from seeing pure color, we should see nothing. Saturation of white hair, all the hues in the cry.

IT IS A QUESTION

WHETHER TOUCH HAS A STONE. And what its organ. A woman with a peacock feather studies the migration of carp. Shirts on a clothesline. How vulnerable the order of civilized achievement. Modes of transport undone in fog. We are not prepared for. The sound of pain, a strident, high-pitched, syncopated melody.

Whether the flesh extends to Iowa. Five senses in the city. In the country, seven. Years itching. Eddies of leaves, color awakened in shuttered light. Even though there is little happiness. And has to be learned like a language.

Whether Adam and Eve could talk, not having clothes. Lips intent only on kiss. No shirts drying from one identity to another. While in respect to the other senses we fall below many species of animals. Though touch is neither good nor evil. Its exact discriminations separate real from world, foreign from body, pleasure from principle.

Whether the keyboard is situated farther inward. In the evening. We must leave before too cold. Before growth and decline are rebuilt as a church. Destination landward. More skin through journeys underground. Organs held in darkness. Against the blue of a fine harvest sky, come down, the tongue.

Whether thought is in danger of. Disappearing inside itself. A smithy in the ear. Categories in the retina. A flapping shirt, a snowfall of face value pointless to fight. Likewise the more genuine part of my life goes by, impossible to define. Flow of breath, the unfolding of a minute, the low notes of pain.

for Peter Gizzi

A STRANGER AND EARLY

TO THIS END, since you've left, I made experiments. Inconclusive sweat ran down my face, my two left hands. Disconsolate, the early morning. The die was cast, the dog's name, Fido.

Opening etymologies and swept away. A current, absolutely distinct from inanimate matter, traversed the view I had taken. Morning rose, a gift of dimensions and potency. Two barges carrying oxygen, glucose, vitamins for metabolism.

I who am all thumbs have discovered, even in spring, the key to the situation. Bound to wind as well as waking. A landlord, a singer, a stocking manufacturer. Near water, as if afraid, in conversation complete with argument. Since then, I find it difficult to face.

Injury above sea level convulses an animal more certainly. But all pleasure. The sky hung with almost regular clouds, as if painted. Some suffered from cold, some from dwindling, but the water level constant.

I became attracted to the utmost. I felt lack like foliage around the arc of the bridge, stone looking like a fruit. Water, my professional secret. But rusty containers along the canals. Who can bear, questioning, wandering, irreversible disorders, two left hands.

The barges moved as if without resistance. If once, the nature of habits and wrinkles. I was like, I was forced, a machine to myself, wide-awake on my iron bed. Shone for me the sun? Surely words are actions: my erection resolved, like sudden joy, explaining often enough.

NOT A DESCRIPTION

ONLY ON SKIN and muscles can we, without harming ourselves, build a symbolic system. She stood at the heart of the matter, holding an egg. A child was being beaten. We recorded everything. Recoded everything. A fish was being eaten. A cry is not a description.

Much of what we observe about the skin. She blushed deeply, perched on the bedpost. Throat parched. We used scientific language without, however, understanding the adjective. She did not want to drop the egg. A cry which cannot be called a description cannot therefore be called swimming in the nude. Tiny fish like silver needles with the current.

Asked point blank, she said a cry was neither a description nor represented in the frontal region. We believed nothing. Conceived nothing. Even with powerful gravitational pull, an angel's complexion resists. She felt a lull in eye movement. Should she go back to sleep? With somebody else's marriage band on her finger?

When the surgeon's knife penetrates the skin, not all persons can be made to look alike. Though given the same pain. If she dropped the egg she would break the dream. Scenes rife with fainting make us want rain. Whales in smooth, hipless motion rising high out of the water. That someone can utter a cry does not mean she can describe the nature of overtones. Or stains linked to association areas.

A cry, which is not a description, is not an image either. Exactly what was removed from her pelvis? The dream narrowed to the fear that comes after. The feel of cold fish scales. Against her skin. Fins out of water. Damage to the battery will affect all connections, whereas damage to a single wire depends on its position in the circuit.

A cry, which is more primitive than a description nevertheless is a description. Heat brought from inside the body to the surface of the skin and rapidly lost. The speed depends on the assembled crowd. The machine's warm parts rest on the floor. The word is not innocent. The dream not interpreted. Not all fibres cross to the opposite side of the brain.

for Elizabeth Willis

83

LIKE MANY OTHERS

I CAME INTO REGRET. The way one enters a place already known. Possibly friendly, traced backwards into convex bodies at the base of the brain. A black dot moves across a screen. The selfpurifying motion of a river. The orange tree bears flowers throughout the year.

A girl in a city. Convolution: maximum surface in smallest possible volume. If I had followed. The street lamps out again. How discover the simple laws of nature? How choose between drama and grammar? Blue jeans rather than tending a tree through summer and winter.

Bearing both fruit and flowers at the same time, the orange is a symbol of purity, fertility and eternal love all at once. Aggregates of neurons. Kids lined up in a red shift, so that the mother's body. Forming basal ganglia. The way I say her name because it is not mine. A girl from the west, a look of perdition, the forest for the trees, and other images from nature.

She eats the fruit hardly allowing it to ripen. Convexities, encoding information from within. Patches of nonsense valuable as nonsense. And repeated four times. Neuronal patterns open to every kind of speculation. What if a girl has enough blood to supply a brain, but scarcely a body?

THE FROG PRINCE

THEY WOULD HAVE IT he was in search of a soul when he only wanted a heart, a hollow bag of muscle, divided into chambers. On his belly. Bodies. Images of bodies. Nostrils, eyes, eardrums and mouth arranged in the same relative positions as in our heads. Prodigious reservoirs.

Why should we need archaic symbols? A head, a trunk, limbs. The girl's mind moves through cavities no longer moist. Dignity consists of separate jointed vertebrae, of right and left hemispheres. The tongue is sticky and can suddenly shoot out of the mouth. No one in Providence remembered such a couple getting married.

Distress squarely in the seat of the soul. Landscape after landscape breaks into a sweat. A great many organs. Frogs swimming through memory, through reservoirs of light. Repetition prefers repetition. Were she foolish enough to ask: Who am I, she would fall flat on her face.

Containing association fibers. So that the brain can function in recoil and advance. Like any other animal, the frog. Prodigious reservoirs of energy, she said, going on living aimlessly. Protruding eyes. Nobody told her the kiss must be repeated.

She diminished in size, but never enough. A disproportion of shadows. She did not ask: am I a monster or what does it mean to be a person? Describing deeper than water. The frog eats, breathes, excretes, moves, mates. But the girl goes back to the baker who fondles her through her dress.

THE WALL

ALL THAT IS never said. In one reunited language. All the rays intersect in the pupil and left becomes right. Without subtitles. In walls we trust. Overstated chemicals in the folds of history. Excited, to the detriment of uncushioned flesh. Drones born of unfertilized eggs. The relation to memory a blind corridor. Footnotes absorbed into blood.

Rays coming from opposite points nevertheless fall on corresponding points of the retina. Like language like wall. Open sky was my heart. Erect carriage, godlike, the void dug by the mirror. We'll find other things to divide us. Wedding bed, touch me not, deterioration in the frontal lobe. The queen bee couples once only. So there is compensation. Can we start over with a taken for granted? With mouths in foreign parts of speech?

Given that reason is ever more lost. The Much Regretted Wall. How get behind the mirror, how use a microscope. Once only, and outside the hive. We localize anatomical areas, ambiguities, applause, aliens. An adjective redesigns fear. Shooting from the abdomen tip, fine as a hair. A mere 20% of the incidents lead to harvest and arrest. Dogs taste milk injected into their bloodstream and begin to lap with their tongues. With only brief surprise between condition and contamination.

So that the eye is placed at the point of greatest confusion. Uniform chemical imperatives. Frustrations that don't hold water. How then comes it to pass, the object being inverted on the fund of the eye, we yet see the object erect? Protein vertigo. Twisted dreams. If point does not correspond to point we feel the ground uncertain and take fright. Photograph over and over, preserve, piece by piece, rub salt into, the shock of the wall.

VOLUNTARY CONTROL

SHE TOUCHED various persons who had their eyes closed or averted. Though their bodies disappointed her, she bowed to the mystery, French at the hips. Was straightway unlaced. Did this rehabilitate childhood? Often only the lower part of the face is afflicted. We must proceed step by step.

Only tactual organs invite catastrophe. She could not settle down to work, but behaved just like anybody. Fingers closing on desire. The moisture of young decimals. Punctuated by claw marks. Normal behavior, a balance of alphabet and straight walls.

As soon as touch evokes pain, an angel approaches the expectant bed. So white a flame that there is no ash and therefore no fertility of fields. Closely savored power line. The fire of terrestrial emotion never so well localized. On her lower-most part. Who uses such language?

A hot, but not quite hatched, temper. Anthropomorphic grammar welcomes all commas. The end of entropy leaning far over the table. Legs thrust under, to balance the additional emotion. The primitive instincts of the child become inhibited and lock the door. The fibres forming this part of the pathway lie deep.

Cold skin more abrupt than abandonment. When she eventually bore a son her knees knocked against. She missed the impermeability of sleep. A wall of withdrawal for homecoming. Laundry waiting to be washed. We cannot expand the concept of "fit" even if we write "dank haze" and "monochrome shadows."

Aroused with a speed the mind can't follow, but seems to ponder. He found maidenheads on various parts of her body. Observation became less accurate. The sources of heat we have within us to appease God, hunger, a lover. "I will dress now," she said. But it was an illusion, a line of mirage over a deep bass counterpoint of failure.

IDENTICAL

HE SAW HIS TWIN DAUGHTERS as one person, their names as portraits. Variables: luminosity, hue, saturation. He told them stories to prevent an expansion of the spectrum. But could he conduct himself like a father?

All that has been figure is now ground, the way a mirror gets behind the subject. The light transcending our limits. Like the harmonic potential of tones. But we do not understand the physiological mechanisms of the simplest memory, such as how to walk.

The eye in the peacock feather sees nothing. Twins are a symbol of the unity of humankind, which they promote by external resemblance. He followed every movement of his hand stroking one daughter's hair.

Composite colors appear less saturated. Their strength lies in spite of opposition. When stored in the cortex. Within the storm, the storm standing still.

A different nerve fiber for each different pitch. The twins moved in two distinct bodies, with identical movements. Such severity persisted for 30 years. Then they confused their father, multiplying their tears as one many times distressed.

Which parts of the ear vibrate with a tone? Which rods, which cones, with the light? Economics, a pressing subject. Though the dead are as represented, a memory.

We cannot precisely ascertain with which feathers a bird feels the coming of a storm. Or love. Since the twins' bodies were alike, their separateness could not be supposed to have the least significance. The father's voice moved through time with an even beat.

He reduced himself to himself. The way a drawing of the nasal labyrinth resolves into male genitals. The way we breathe and smell. A base line in a score.

Both twins were called Marie. Their almost same appearance made them expect the same opportunities and happiness. The father pronounced his vowels with care lest a tremor crack them. Lest the crucial indifference of numbers come to the surface.

MORNING'S INTELLIGENCE

1

One night I thought of drinking
elsewhere

a deep draft of beginning
reveling in the instant

as if it
could never age

you said in a dream
"I have invented the cinema
no doubt it has a future"

intent
        on being naked
pores burst open
senses laced
into forgetting distinctions

where I come from
the apples

and I ate and ate

2

happiness is round
                         fills
what it enters
a simple time
opening toward quiet like fishing

it made us
predictable
                    a catch

between us and where
we come from

for instance the same gesture
again and again into sleep
dial of water

so thin a line whispering
the loss of direction

3

sleep thick with
planetary fragments float in space
and friction

a tiny
sunburst in your eyes

where need is blind
interpretations grow

already the clouds

I imagine
I can see it still
though the long
silence
obscures your body

4

closer than any
the soft sliding

begins between two points of cold

a different darkness
flat
against the mirror

I worried your skin like a page of braille
nothing
could be deciphered

then a whole body of air
went out the chimney
narrow breath
no concession to the ground

5

had it been light

you
with disconcerting ease
withdrew into circumstance

and to think that the height of mountains
is constantly worn down

silence erupts
in riddles we both understand

6

to stay embedded against the dawn
of matter and fact

then only the unfit items
a laugh to represent bad timing
or tears where anyone
could use a joke

the air this side of perspective
the missing links
a hardness where focus

you've already taken
the distance I thought of
and it not noon

false notes:
connect them into evidence
abridged seduction

someday comedy
will reinvent
this situation

meanwhile we can watch the cows
chew on their indifference

7

wet pavement
all spring long no ceiling
on clouds

elsewhere the vessels connect

bodies skidding toward
their margin

vertiginous cliffs, you said
skin's
our last prayer
folds into grey matter, so
little time

8

your voice a shadow
out of the last light year
split echo
under the skin

how it eats inward

spring
of course spring
no other season would have fostered
this smell of jasmin

where I come from
the real dark
tears through the valley the trees

of course
you can't without

you have no body now

9

can we still
replace our meeting
with the recent rain

late is
incomprehensible

an increase
in the weight of air
the moment before

fitful sleep
oversize islands
in the breath

10

thin morning
the air conditional, grey

before
I could recite the alphabet
as well as you

now drift, unwelcome
reflections, shifts into

look at my sweater
I wear it
instead of skin

line visible
between and

city made of wet windows
I might think a lake and sink
drop by drop
through a space I'd thought
deliberate

more likely looking toward
sky erased by lack of birds

11

all too slowly the light

if a map does not chart
the already discovered

remains hunger

you must open your legs
inside the muscles

it's there
the ground between us
has folded on its conclusion

only the words keep
pushing
their own pale violence

SINGING HORSE PRESS TITLES

Ammiel Alcalay, *the cairo notebooks*. 1993, $9.50.
Asa Benveniste, *Invisible Ink*. 1989, $4.00.
Charles Bernstein, *Artifice of Absorption*. 1987, $5.00.
Julia Blumenreich, *Meeting Tessie*. 1994, $6.00.
Linh Dinh, *Drunkard Boxing*. 1998, $8.00.
Rachel Blau DuPlessis, *Draft X: Letters*. 1990, $6.00.
Robert Fitterman, *Among the Cynics*. 1989, OP.
Karen Kelley, *Her Angel*. 1992, $7.50.
Kevin Killian/Leslie Scalapino, *Stone Marmalade*. 1996, $9.50
Kush, *The End Befallen Edgar Allen Poe*. 1982, $2.00.
David Miller, *Unity*. 1981, $3.00.
Harryette Mullen, *Muse & Drudge*. 1995, $12.50.
Harryette Mullen, *S*PeRM**K*T*. 1992, $8.00.
Gil Ott, *Traffic (Books I & II)*. 1985, $2.50.
Ted Pearson, *Soundings*. 1980, OP.
Rosmarie Waldrop, *Differences for Four Hands*. 1984, OP.
Rosmarie Waldrop, *Split Infinites*. 1998, $14.00.
Craig Watson, *Drawing A Blank*. 1980, OP.
Vassilis Zambaras, *Aural*. 1984, $2.00.